Winter Crochet:

25 Superb Crochet Scarves, Hats and Gloves for Your Warm Comfort

Easy, quick and fun-to-make patterns

CU01507499

Disclamer: All photos used in this book, including the cover photo were made available under a Attribution-NonCommercial-ShareAlike 2.0 Generic and sourced from Flickr

Table of Contents

Introduction

If you have always wanted to try out crocheting in your free time, there is no better moment than the present. All over the world, there are millions of people who share the same passion, creating amazing products with their own hands. Many of the handmade items have been offered as gifts and, let us face it, everyone loves a gift that is personalized.

The good news is that you have the opportunity to create amazing accessories for the cold winter season. Elegant and stylish, the patterns are available not only for scarves but also for hats and gloves.

You can create a complete set and offer to a precious someone as a lovely gift. As for the materials that you need, these are not complicated at all. Basically, you need the yarn, the crochet hook (of various sizes), yarn needle and a pair of scissors.

In the pages that follow, you will discover beautiful patterns, meant to fill your free time in a relaxed and fun manner. Do not hesitate to try out all of them and create amazing accessories that everyone loves to wear.

Chapter 1 – Easy & quick crochet scarves

If you are passionate about crocheting in general, you will definitely love to create the following scarves patterns. Keep in mind that these scarves represent perfect accessories for the cold season.

Moreover, when done, you can offer them as a gift to someone you love. Keep on reading, in order to discover easy and quick crochet scarves patterns.

#1 Beginner's crochet scarf

This is a simple crochet scarf pattern to follow, definitely recommended for beginners. For this scarf, you will need these supplies: 200 yards of yarn, crochet hook size I, crochet needle and scissors. You can begin by adding a slipknot to your crochet hook, crocheting no less than 13 chain stitches.

After that, chain stich three more stitches, as these are going to represent your first double crochet. What you want to do next is count five loops from the edge, performing a double crochet in that fifth loop (this will represent the second stitch on that row). Make a double crochet for each loop, until you reach the end of the row. Repeat the process so as to obtain 13 stitches for each row (first chain of three included).

Turn the yarn over and repeat until you reach the length you desire. When you have finished the scarf, all you have to do is cut the yarn, pulling it through the last loop. Then, hide the tail using the crochet needle.

#2 Braided crochet scarf

If you are looking for a scarf that is easy to make but also unique to wear, the braided crochet pattern is exactly what you need. For this pattern, you will need similar supplies with the ones mentioned above. Begin with a number of chain stitches and, remember, you can go as far as 100, depending on how long you want the actual scarf to be. Then, perform a double crochet back on the chain. The process of double crocheting should be repeated for a number of five rows (chain not included). Once you are done with the first mini scarf, proceed with the same steps and create the other two.

When you have made all three, all you have to do is braid them together. For the final step, sew the ends together, transforming it into an infinity scarf. Tip: you can use different yarn colors for a bolder look.

#3 Chunky crochet cowl

For the making of this unique accessory, all you need is chunky yarn and a crochet hook. As you will have the opportunity to read below, this is quick to make and not complicated at all.

Start by chaining 45 stitches and, when you reach the end of the chain, make sure that it is straightened. Then, slip the stitch through the initial chain and perform three more chains. For the first row, perform a double crochet into the fifth stitch.

Then, repeat the process for each of the stitches present in the respective row. As you reach the final part of the row, the stitch should be slipped through the superior part of the first chain of three. In this way, you will join the circle. Repeat the same steps for all rows, until you obtain the desired length. When done, all you have to do is tie the end and cut the yarn. Then, hide the tail with the help of the crochet needle.

#4 Round shell stitch cowl

This pattern is beautiful and elegant at the same time, not to mention extremely easy to do. For the making of this cowl, you will have to crochet in round, starting with the initial chains. Once you have made these, the stitch will have to be slipped through the first chain, so as to form a circle.

Then, you will practically work the shell stitches in round. When the last stitch in a row has been completed, you will reach the first stitch that was made in the initial phase. In order to close the row, you will have to perform a slip stich, reaching the top of the initial chain (made in the beginning).

Then, you will connect with the next stich. The process will have to be repeated, so as the shell stitches appear to be one on top of the other. The pattern will have to be completed for all 13 rounds.

#5 Infinity scarf

Infinity scarves are popular at the moment, as they have a pattern that is quick and easy to make. If you are looking to create a scarf that will keep you warm during the cold winter season, the infinity scarf is your number one choice.

For the making of this scarf, you will need two skeins of bulky weight yarn, an 8-mm crochet hook and yarn needles. Start the pattern with 25 chain stiches. For the first row, work single crochet for each chain space, then turn.

Continue on the second row, with double crochet and turn. In the third row, you should work single crochet for each of the double crochet loops, turning as well. For the forth row, you should work single crochet for each of the chain spaces, turning at the end. These steps should be repeated until you reach the desired length for the scarf.

#6 Powdered sugar crochet infinity scarf

Speaking about infinity scarves, you will definitely love this particular one. This is a great choice for beginners and it requires 2 yarn skeins and a 10-mm crochet hook. In the situation that you want to make it in the round, you will have to chain 74, then perform the slip stich to join, chain 1.

Then, round one, until you would have used all of the yarn. It is single crochet all around, so there is no need to join the rounds or actually count them. You can also try flat crocheting. Chain 16, then perform single crochet for the first row and turn. Row two until you have used all the yarn. When done, sew the ends together.

#7 Crochet rib scarf

The crochet rib scarf can keep you warm during the cold winter days and help you look stylish at the same time. This pattern is performed using the single crochet stitch and it requires 2 yarn skeins, a 10-mm crochet hook and a large-eyed blunt needle.

Start with chain 121, then, for the first row, perform the single crochet in second chain from hook. The single crochet should also be performed in each chain across, so that you have 120 single crochets at the end of the row. For the second row, chain 1, turn and work in back loops.

Then, perform single crochet for each single crochet across. Repeat the second row until you reach the desired length. Weave the ends in order to finish the scarf.

#8 Arugula scarf

The great thing about the Arugula scarf is that it is lightweight, being recommended for any time of the year. For the making of this scarf, you will require: 5-mm crochet hook, ½ skein and tapestry needle.

The latter is necessary for weaving in the ends of the scarf. Chain 200, then proceed to foundation row. Double crochet at the fourth chain from the hook, then you should perform one double crochet for each chain, until you reach the end of the row.

In the first row, turn, then chain three and perform a double crochet for the first stitch (and also for the other stitches, until you reach the end of the row). Repeat the first row two more times and then proceed to the ruffle row.

Turn, chain three and perform three double stitches for the first stitch. Repeat the procedure for the entire row. Weave in the ends with the tapestry needle.

#9 Quick cowl scarf

If you are looking for a scarf that can be created in under an hour, this is the perfect choice for you to make. All you need is a 9-mm crochet hook, 1 yarn skein and you are set to go. Chain 74, then join together in the round, using the slip stitch.

The first row, chain three, then work treble crochet for each chain space around. Join using the slip stitch and proceed to second row. Chain two and work double crochet in the treble crochet spaces that belong to the previous spaces. Join and move to third row.

Chain one, performing single crochet across in the double crochet spaces of the second row. Join and go to row four. Chain three and perform treble crochet in the single crochet spaces of the previous row. Join and reach row five.

Chain one and perform single crochet in treble crochet spaces of the last row. Join and go to the sixth row. Chain two, then double crochet in the single crochet spaces of the previous row. Join and go to the seventh row. Chain one and perform single crochet for the entire row. Join with slip stich and done.

Chapter 2 – Beautiful & stylish crochet hats

Crochet hats are wonderful to pair up with the crochet scarves you have created. So, if you want to have a complete set, do not hesitate to try out the suggestions that have been included in this chapter. As you will have the opportunity to read on your own, these are easy to make and they look beautiful in the end.

#1 Basic beanie

The beanie is one of the easiest types of hats to crochet, which makes it an ideal choice for beginners. For this pattern, you will need: scissors, F crochet hook and medium-weight yarn.

Begin by creating a loop with the help of the crochet hook. Then, the crochet hook will have to go through the loop. The next step will be to create five chains, pulling the yarn over the hook and through the loop.

Once you have created the five chains, all you have to do is make a slip stich into the initial chain. In order to do that, the hook will have to be inserted through the first chain, followed by the wrapping of the yarn around the hook and pulling the yarn into the loop. After the slip stich has been made, 10 double crochets will be made, marking the end of the first round.

For the second round, stitch three double crochets in each double crochet around. The next four rounds will have two double crochets in each double crochet around. The last eight rounds will have single double crochets in each double crochet around.

#2 Quick crochet hat

If you are looking for a hat that is fun and quick to make, this is the perfect pattern to try out. For this pattern, you will need: a 10-mm crochet hook, yarn needle and yarn.

Chain four and join with a slip stitch, in order to form a ring. Chain three, 11 double crochet into the above-mentioned ring; then, join with a slip stitch in top of chain three. For the second round, chain three, front post double crochet around joining stitch 11 times; then, join with a slip stitch in top of chain three.

For the third round, chain three, double crochet in joining stitch, front post double crochet around the front post double crochet 11 times; then, join. In the fourth round, chain three, skip the actual joining of the stitch, double crochet in double crochet, front post double crochet around front post double crochet 11 times and then join.

For the next five rounds, repeat the steps in the fourth round. For round eleven through fifteen, chain three, skin joining the stitch and front post double crochet around each stitch around, then join. Weave in the ends.

#3 Unisex crochet hat

You might not have thought about it but it is possible to create a unisex crochet hat that look fantastic. For this pattern you will need medium-worsted weight yarn and a 5-mm crochet hook.

For the first row, chain 45. In the second row, single crochet in each chain's back loop, until you have only five chains remaining. You will skip the last five stitches at every four rows. Chain one, then turn. For the third row, single crochet in each chain's back loop, until you reach the end of the row. Chain one, then turn. For the fourth row, repeat the third row's process, including the five chains that you initially skipped.

Chain one, then turn. For the fifth row, single crochet in each chain's back loop, until you reach the end of the row. Chain one, then turn. Repeat the rows until you reach the desired length. Sew the seam of the hat with a yarn needle. Then, weave in the ends.

#4 Slouchy crochet hat

The slouchy hat is stylish and can be worn as an accessory to various outfits. For this pattern, you will need one yarn skein and a size J hook. Start with a slipknot.

Chain four, then use the slip stich in order to form a circle. Round two, chain two, twelve half double crochet inside the created circle, slip stitch. Round three, chain two, two half double crochet, half double crochet one and repeat, slip stitch (by now, 18 stitches). Round four, chain two, repeat the above step (24 stitches). Round five, chain two, then repeat (30 stitches).

Repeat the same for sixth and seventh round (42 stitches). For round eight, chain two, puff nine, two puff and repeat. Repeat the same for round nine, then, for rounds 10 to 16, perform one puff stitch for each of the stitches. For round 17, single crochet in each of the stitches.

Round 18, single crochet five, single crochet decrease and repeat. Same process for round 19. Round 20, single crochet for each stitch. Tie off and weave in the ends.

#5 Easy-to-make crochet hat

While there are many crochet hat patterns out there, not all of them are easy to make. This pattern is easy to make and it does not occupy too much of your time. So, for this crochet hat, you will require a 4.5 mm crochet hook and yarn. If you want the hat to be a little bit slouchy, chain 40.

Begin your pattern with the initial chain and, remember, this will dictate the size of the actual hat. Single crochet into the second chain from the hook and repeat the same process for the other chains. Chain one, turn the work and then single crochet for each of the stitches.

Repeat the rows until you reach the desired length. Fasten the ends. Sew the top if you want the hole to close completely. Whip stitch the sides of the hat and you are done.

#6 French beret

The French beret is an elegant accessory to create, so it is definitely worth your time. For this pattern, you will require: 10-mm crochet hook, bulky yarn, scissors and wool needle.

Begin your work with a slipknot and chain 28 chains. For the first row, chain two, crochet one half double crochet into the fourth chain. Continue with a half double crochet (for the next four chains) and then with double crochet (for the next fourteen chains).

Return to the half double crochet for the next four chains. Continue with the single crochet for the next four chains (28 stitches by now). For the second row, crochet one slip stitch into every stitch across.

For the third row, chain two and crochet one half double crochet into the next five stitches' back loop. Continue with a double crochet for the next fourteen stitches. For the next four stitches, half double crochet and single crochet for the four ones that follow.

For the fourth row, crochet one slip stitch into every stitch across. The fifth row is identical to the third row. Repeat the third and fourth rows, until you reach the desired length. Fasten off and weave in the ends. Thread the yarn through the end rows, using the tapestry needle. Close the hole and make a pom-pom using bulky yarn as well.

#7 Winter crochet hat

The cold season is the perfect time to wear unique accessories, such as the hat that can be created with this pattern. Moreover, this is a simple pattern, which makes it more than suitable for beginners.

All you need is yarn and a size I crochet hook. Begin with 46 chains. For the first row, half double crochet in the back loop of the second chain from the hook and in each chain across. Chain one, then turn.

For the rows two to thirty-five, half double crochet for each back loop of the chain. Chain one, then turn. Row 36, repeat the process and then fasten off. Weave in the ends. If you want, you can attach a pom-pom to your newly-made hat.

#8 Ear flap hat

Ear flap hats are perfect for a sporty look, also keeping you warm during the cold winter season. For the making of this pattern, you will need the following supplies: worsted weight yarn (1 skein), 5-mm crochet hook and yarn needle.

Begin with the actual hat, then you will create the flaps. For the first round, chain two, perform eight half double crochet in the second chain from the hook, then join in the first half double crochet.

For the second round, chain one, then make two half double crochet in each stitch around and join. In the third round, chain one, make two half double crochet for the first stitch and a half double crochet for the next stitch. Repeat around and then join. Round four to eight, repeat the same process, only for an increasing number of stitches (by one).

Round nine, repeat for 15 stitches. Round 10 to 22, chain one and perform half double crochet for each stitch.

For the first ear flap, join in the tenth stitch from the initial seam. For the first row, chain one, single crochet in the same stitch and single crochet for the next eleven stitches, then turn. Row two to ten, chain one, skip the first stitch, single crochet for the next stitch and in each stitch across, then turn. Row eleven, chain one, skip the first stitch, single crochet for the next three stitches, then fasten off.

For the second ear flap, join in at the twenty-sixth stitch. Repeat the same steps as for the first, without fastening off after the last row. Instead, work around the hat and make single crochet for each stitch, including the end of each row of the ear flaps. Fasten off and weave in the ends.

Chapter 3 – Fun & stylish crochet gloves

When it's cold outside, it is only normal that you should wear gloves. Crochet gloves are perfect for all kinds of weather, protecting your hands against the unwanted effects of low temperatures. Below, you will find fun & stylish crochet gloves patterns. Have fun while trying them!

#1 Easy-to-make fingerless crochet gloves

This is a pattern recommended for those who are trying to make their very first pair of crochet gloves. You can begin by chaining as many stitches as it is necessary to cover your hand. Then, continue by stitching as many rows as you desire, between the glove's top and the actual thumbhole.

When you begin a new row, fold the work, so as to identify the exact location of the thumbhole. In order for the seam to be near the little finger, you need to stitch up the spot for the thumbhole.

Then, chain off of the row, going around the thumb. The hook should be pushed through the stitch and then you continue the work. Continue to create rows, according to how long you want the gloves to be. When done, fold the work in half and stitch it up on the lateral sides. All done!

#2 One-hour wrist warmers

Everyone loves wrist warmers, as they are lovely to wear, yet highly functional. So, if you are looking for a quick crochet project to try out, this is perfect. As supplies, you will need: 2 oz. worsted weight yarn, size G crochet hook and yarn needle. Chain 24, slip stitch to the first chain in order to close the loop. For the first round, chain one, half double crochet in each chain around, slip stitch to the first half double crochet in order to join.

For round two to five, chain one, half double crochet in each stitch around, slip stitch to the first half double crochet to join. Round six, chain one, half double crochet in each stitch around, no need to join, chain one and turn.

Round seven to nine, half double crochet in each stitch around, chain one and turn. Round ten, half double crochet in each stitch across, slip stitch to first half double crochet to join. Round eleven to eighteen, chain one, half double crochet in each stitch around, slip stitch to first half double crochet to join. Fasten off and weave in the ends.

#3 Vintage fingerless gloves

If you are looking for a vintage look, this pattern is a must-try. For the making of these gloves, you will require the following supplies: 4.5-mm crochet hook, yarn, scissors and tapestry needle, 40 cm ribbon (optional). Start by making a slipknot and then chain 30 stitches.

The first chain should be joined with a slip stitch. First row, chain two, half double crochet in each chain around, then slip stitch to the second chain of the stitch. Row 2 to 6, chain two, half double crochet in every stitch around, then join with slip stitch to the second chain. Row 7, chain two, half double crochet for the next nine stitches. Now, make the hole for the thumb.

Chain four, then skip four stitches. Half double crochet for the stitches that remain. Join with slip stitch to the second chain. Rows 8 to 15, chain two, half double crochet in each chain around, then join with slip stitch. Row 16, turn the work, chain three, double crochet into the first stitch.

Slip stitch to the following stitch. Make the edge by yarning over, inserting the hook through the next stitch, yarning over and pulling back through the stitch. Repeat the process until you complete the ends. Fasten off and weave in the ends. Place a ribbon through the stitches at the bottom for a more vintage look.

#4 Puff stitch fingerless gloves

The puff stitch fingerless gloves are beautiful and stylish, so go ahead and give this pattern a try. For this pattern, you will need the following supplies: 4.5-mm crochet hook, wool, wool needle and scissors.

For the wrist ribbing, start by making a slipknot and chain 32 stitches. First row, push the crochet hook into the second chain, then single crochet the entire row. Second row, chain two, push the hook into the second last single crochet. Single crochet the entire row. Third row, the same. Row four, same as 2nd row, until you have only four stitches left.

Crochet two chain stitches, skip to stitches and push the hook through the second last stitch. Single crochet for the remaining two stitches. Rows 5 to 7, same as 2nd row. Row 8, same as row 4. Row 9-12, same as row 2. Fasten off and weave in the ends. Add buttons if you want.

For the hand, being the first row with a slip knot. Push the crochet hook through the overlapping wrist ribbings. Crochet single crochet all around the ribbing. Second row, crochet puff stitches.

Rows 3-4, puff stitch, chain two, skip one stitch. Repeat. Row 5, add the hole for the thumb. Rows 6-8, the same as third row. Row 9-10, single crochet the entire row. Fasten off and weave in the ends.

#5 Bullion stitch fingerless gloves

Fingerless gloves are a fashionable choice and the bullion stitch definitely adds a note of elegance. For this pattern, you will require: 5-mm crochet hook, thick needle, yarn, scissors and tapestry needle.

For the cuff, make a slipknot and crochet 27 chain stitches. First row, push the crochet hook into the second chain from the hook. Single crochet the entire row. Second row, chain two, then push the crochet into the second chain. Single crochet the entire row.

For the hand, first row, chain one, then single crochet the entire row and join with a slip stitch. Rows 2-4, chain three, then crochet the bullion stitch into the following stitch.

Chain one, skip one stitch and repeat the bullion stitch. Repeat across the entire row and join with a slip stitch (top of chain three). Row five, add the hole for the thumb. Row 6, same as row 2. Row 7-8, same as row 2. Row 9-10, single crochet across the entire row(s). Fasten off and weave in the ends.

#6 Princess fingerless gloves

This is a basic pattern but one that will deliver an amazing pair of gloves in the end. For this pattern, you will need: 5-mm crochet hook, 4.5-mm crochet hook, yarn, tapestry needle and scissors. For the cuff, make a slip knot with the 5-mm crochet hook. Chain 13 chain stitches, single crochet into the second chain from the hook. Repeat for the entire row.

For left hand, first row, use the 4.5-mm crochet hook. Chain one, single crochet around the entire row and join with a slip stitch. Second row, chain one, then single crochet for the next two stitches. Crochet single crochet the rest of the row. Join with a slip stitch. Third row, chain one, crochet a single crochet in the first stitch, then two single crochets for the next two stitches.

Crochet single crochet the entire row and join with a slip stitch. Fourth row, chain one, single crochet first two stitches, two single crochet next two stitches, single crochet the entire row. Join with a slip stitch. Row five, chain one, single crochet first three stitches, then the same as above. Row 6-10, chain one, single crochet the entire row and join with slip stitch. Row 11, chain five, skin 11 stitches and single crochet in the next stitch.

Single crochet the entire row without joining. Rows 12-19, single crochet around the cuff, not around the thumb hole. Slip stitch, then fasten off. For the right hand, simply mirror the steps recommended for the left hand.

#7 Wrist warmers with ridges

If you want a pair of gloves that will leave your fingers free, while keeping your wrist and arms warm, this is the ideal pattern to try out. These are the materials that you will require: medium-weight yarn, 5.5-mm crochet hook and yarn needle.

The pattern is presented for one wrist warmer, so you will have to repeat it in order to obtain a complete set. First row, chain 41 chain stitches, the second crochet in the second chain from the hook and in each chain across.

Second row, turn your work, single crochet in the back loop of each chain. Repeat the second row, until you reach the desired length for your wrist warmers. Using the yarn needle, sew the sides together. All done!

#8 Fingerless gloves for men

If you are looking for a nice gift to offer to your husband, you can create a pair of fingerless gloves yourself. This pattern is incredibly easy to make and, most importantly, does not require too much of your time.

As supplies, you will need: medium weight yarn, 5-mm crochet hook and yarn needle. The pattern is presented for one glove, so you will have to repeat it in order to obtain the second glove.

First row, chain 34 chain stitches, then double crochet in third chain from the hook and double crochet in each chain across. For the second row, chain two, turn your work, then double crochet in each chain across. Use the yarn needle in order to sew the sides of the glove together. Now it is gift-giving time!

Conclusion

Here you are at the end of the book. It has been an amazing journey, allowing you to discover beautiful patterns for scarves, hats and gloves. With the winter season in full bloom, it kind of makes sense to sit cozily in your home and crochet the time away.

Moreover, these patterns can be adapted and used to create accessories for the entire family, whether we are talking about children, mums or dads. Plus, it is guaranteed that these are perfect gifts to offer to the ones you love.

Always remember that crocheting is more than a hobby or a way to spend your free time. It is a way to create beautiful accessories, for the people that mean the world to you. Whether you make a beanie hat for your little lady or some fingerless gloves for your man, it is guaranteed that you will have an amazing time while crocheting.

And, be sure, it is great to see an actual scarf/hat/glove coming out of your very own hands!

FREE Bonus Reminder

If you have not grabbed it yet, please go ahead and download your special bonus report *"DIY Projects. 13 Useful & Easy To Make DIY Projects To Save Money & Improve Your Home!"*

Simply Click the Button Below

OR **Go to This Page**

http://diyhomecraft.com/free

BONUS #2: More Free Books

Do you want to receive more Free Books?

We have a mailing list where we send out our new Books when they go free on Kindle. Click on the link below to sign up for Free Book Promotions.

=> Sign Up for Free Book Promotions <=

OR Go to this URL

http://zbit.ly/1WBb1Ek

Printed in Great Britain
by Amazon

54467211R00020